15 Foolproof Strategies to Successfully Survive Unemployment & Rebuild Your Life & Finances

15 Foolproof Strategies to Successfully Survive Unemployment & Rebuild Your Life & Finances

Get Your Life Back Into Full Bloom!

- Financially & Otherwise

Heidi E. Vincent

Heidi Eunice Vincent
2015

ISBN: 978-1-329-37521-5 (Paperback edition)

ISBN: 978-1-329-35909-3 (eBook edition)

Published by Heidi Eunice Vincent

Perdmontemps P.O., St. David, Grenada, West Indies.

www.thecatholiccontributor.com

This book is dedicated to **Almighty God**,

for His continuous love and provision during my season of

unemployment

and to some wonderful people (more than friends),

who helped me keep my head above the stormy waters -

Lueandra & Lyndon, Annamay & Clifford (R.I.P),

Isaac & Najmie, Lisa

May God bless you all abundantly!!!

"A loyal friend is like a safe shelter; find one, and you have found a treasure. Nothing else is as valuable; there is no way of putting a price on it. A loyal friend is like a medicine that keeps you in good health. Only those who fear the Lord can find such a friend" ~ *Sirach 6:13-16.*

Table of Contents

Prologue

I love collecting quotes but the main criteria for a quote finding its way into my personal little 'Book of Quotes & Wise Sayings', is that it must resonate with me and impart some profound wisdom about life and living. One of my favourite and, I must add, very apt quotes came to mind as I reflected on my past 5 years plus of unemployment:

> *"Life is like a minefield we all walk through.*
> *The only thing we know for certain is that we'll all be hit.*
> *The question is when and how badly we'll be hurt, and more importantly, how well we'll recover from our wounds."*
>
> **'Wise Women Speak to Women Turning 30'**, by *Jean Aziz, Peggy Stout & Marie Bode*

As I write this book, I am still licking my unemployment wounds but I have to admit that I have come to understand and appreciate life and its varied experiences so much more. I have also gained some wisdom about weathering unemployment that I needed to impart to others. No psychologist or therapist, no matter how good she/he is, can convey this kind of wisdom to you, especially if she/he has never actually been unemployed.

No-one can prepare you for what you will face and endure as first the days, then the months and then the years of unemployment roll by. However, as a Christian, I have taken to heart the wisdom spoken by St. Paul in 2 Corinthians 1:4:

"[God] helps us in all our troubles, so that we are able to help others who have all kinds of troubles, using the same help that we ourselves have received from God."

Somewhere out there in our 'big-tiny' world, you or someone you know is currently struggling with unemployment, underemployment or irregular employment and finding it hard to cope from day to day, minute to minute. So I'll share with you, from my personal experience, how I coped with and survived unemployment and I hope it blesses all who read it, share it and use it!

I praise God for his continuous help! May God Bless, in a very special way, all those who helped me financially and otherwise during those difficult years!

Introduction

"A crisis is an opportunity in disguise. A solution is hidden in the folds of every reverse.
No matter what is thrown into our face, there is a way to roll with the punch."
~ Sri Harold Klemp

I was sure of it! Within 6 months, or 1 year for the most, I would find another great paying job, my Business Consultancy would be well established, since I had a really great track record of doing excellent work, and my life and finances would be right back on track again.

But as the months rolled by, instead I found myself facing difficulties with meeting my monthly mortgage loan and vehicle loan obligations. I saw my savings in my bank account and other investment accounts dwindle and vanish. Finding another full-time job just about anywhere in the world became my priority.

I remember crying my heart out one night as I faced the hard truth that the next morning, bright and early, I would have to reach out for help. It was a heart-rending decision for me because I have always been a very organized and independent person and I had, up until then, successfully taken care of myself and my finances. In fact, I had a Master's degree in Finance. *(Oh, the irony of life!)*

1

But at that particular point in my life, I just could not hold it together financially on my own any longer, with little or no money coming in.

I say little or no money because I would sporadically *(once a year)* get a short-term consultancy *(about 10 days)* but by the time I received payment for my services, the money would all be eaten up in back dated bills, expenses and credit card debts I had incurred from just buying groceries to eat on a monthly basis.

On one occasion, I was without running water for 4 months. On top of all that was happening financially, I had an underground water leak that sent my water bill through the roof ($500). Nevertheless, I had tried to meet my monthly water bill while adding a little something each month to pay off for the leak. I thought things were moving along quite well until the water company decided that it was the end of the financial year and that I was taking too long to pay off the debt. So, despite me explaining that I was unemployed, that my records could show that I was paying something, no matter how small, my water was disconnected.

On another occasion, during the Christmas season, I was doing my best to avoid letting my deteriorated financial position get to me. So I put on some Christmas music to lift my spirits and went about cleaning out my home. Suddenly, I heard knocking on my front door. I went to answer the door and found an employee from the electricity company. He delivered a written notice to me that my electricity would be cut off in 2 days due to some overdue electricity bills.

Now all this was extremely traumatic for a person like me, who, prior to being unemployed always paid my bills on time, had several saving accounts and managed my money and other people's money quite efficiently, as a financial professional.

Like I said earlier, I firmly believe that *"[God] helps us in all our troubles, so that we are able to help others who have all kinds of troubles, using the same help that we ourselves have received from God."* (2 Corinthians 1:4)

I have received tremendous help from God, through the various persons he strategically placed in my path and some of the strongest friendships that he established long before I dreamed of ever falling into a financial crisis.

So the primary reason I am writing this book, is so that it can be a blessing to you or someone you know who is currently grappling with the effects of unemployment, underemployment or sporadic unemployment and wondering how and if they are going to survive and see better days ahead.

The **15 Unemployment Survivor Strategies** that I will share in this book reveal some of my very own personal experiences and struggles. Depending on how long you've been unemployed to date, 1 day or 5 years, you may be able to relate to my various experiences in your current situation and find some comfort in the knowledge that this has happened to others before you and that you will make it through and see better days.

May your latter be greater than your past!

Survivor Strategy 1

Don't Depend on That One Golden Egg from the Golden Goose

"Never depend on a single income. Make Investments to create a second source."
~ Warren Buffet

If you don't already know it, Warren Buffet is a multi-billionaire and, based on my unemployment experience, this is one of his best life tips that I would advise, everyone, at whatever stage of life you are at, to take very much to heart.

You see, many people who are in good salaried jobs that pay really well, like I was, often make the mistake of depending solely on that one great paying job, much like their golden egg from the golden goose. **What happens, however, when you no longer have that great paying job?** Well I know what I am speaking about because I found myself in that very predicament.

Some of us know and practice the principle of not putting all of our eggs in one basket when it comes to savings. However, as it relates to income generation, most of us haven't transferred that knowledge to our income earning. We have failed to practice the very powerful principle of having multiple income generating sources.

5

The world has changed with respect to employment and how employers see employees. In my parents' working years, employees were hell bent on keeping their valued employees for a lifetime and most hardworking employees were safe in the knowledge that they had a lifetime job and would receive a pension at the end of their working years upon retirement.

In our fast-paced, modern world, many companies and organizations are moving away from employing full-time employees. Most times, persons are issued with a 2 or 3-year contract that is subject to renewal at the employer's whim and fancy.

Another new employment trend that has quickly become the norm is that of replacing full-time jobs with temporary and part-time positions. All of these employment tactics are being embraced by employers in an effort to reduce the wage bill and cut out long-term costs such as insurance, medical plans & pensions.

Once it began to sink in that I would have to find creative ways to generate income in order to survive financially, I began looking online for opportunities. One such opportunity was as an online writer for Squidoo *(Squidoo has since been bought over by Hubpages)*. I joined Squidoo in April 2012, having been unemployed for almost 2 years, and by the time Squidoo was bought over by Hubpages in 2014, I had written 138 articles.

I have written on various topic areas including, art & craft projects that you can attempt yourself, Catholic issues, Christianity, book reviews, cooking recipes, music and movie reviews, gift ideas, health & fitness, games & toys, personal development, etc. You can find all of my varied articles at http://heidivincent.hubpages.com

How writing online at Squidoo worked is that I got paid mainly based on the ranking of my articles and a commission on items that persons purchased online, from Amazon, eBay and Zazzle, while on my article pages.

At first, I only made a few cents per month and then I started earning a few dollars. Some persons I know earned much more than I did with online writing; enough to pay for short staycation trips or a Disney World trip. Whether you make it big doing online writing or earn a few dollars, like me, the point is that it all adds up and when you're unemployed, a little money is better than no money.

What's also really great about online writing, and online teaching which I also did part-time, is that you don't have to be in a particular country to do them. You can write or teach from anywhere in the world that you live and right from the comfort of your very own home.

What YOU Can Do! – Get Started on Survivor Strategy No. 1

Apply the principle of generating multiple income sources. I wish I had applied this principle earlier but it is 'better late than never'. Here's some of what I did and what you can do too:

1. Write online articles on just about any topic that interests you *(I wrote for Squidoo which was later bought over by Hubpages. There are lots of other online companies looking for good writing on just about any topic).*

2. Become an affiliate marketer for a company like Amazon. As an Amazon Associate, you can sell Amazon products for a commission *(4% to 6.5% depending on your monthly sales volume).*

3. Start a website about something you are passionate about and link to related products from Amazon, as an Amazon Associate *(I started **The Catholic Contributor** website - http://www.thecatholiccontributor.com - to solve everyday issues for Catholics and Christians from*

a Christian perspective; from music, to gift giving to pornography).

4. Give private classes or lessons to students *(most students between the ages of 10 and 16 often need help with various subject areas).*

5. Teach online *(most Universities currently have an online component and require a Master's degree as the minimum qualification for teaching in their online program).*

6. Invigilate for secondary or university school examinations.

7. Become a network marketer *(I sell people the opportunity to start their own business and drink quality hot beverages – green tea and coffee infused with a powerful Asian healing herb called Ganoderma Lucidum. You can visit me at* http://heidivincentgrenada.myorganogold.com *).*

8. Start your own business in an area that you love and have good knowledge and skills *(I started my own Business/Management Consultancy – Quality Solutions for Business Excellence which you can visit at* https://sites.google.com/site/qsbeconsultancy *).*

9. Write an eBook on a subject you love, are passionate about or have extensive experience and knowledge about and sell it online through Kindle

Direct Publishing or any of the other free self-publishing companies online.

May God bless you with steady and sustainable income!

Survivor Strategy 2
Grow Your Own Vegetables and Seasonings &/or Buy Local

> *"**Buy Local - Support Yourself** – Local business strengthens the economic base of every community. A good deal of the dollars spent with local businesses is used to make purchases from other local entities - creating a domino effect that can preserve a neighborhood even in an economic slowdown."* ~ Buy Local Campaign Pleasanton

I became unemployed on July 1, 2010 and my Dad died in December 2010; a devastating combination! I gave the eulogy at his funeral mass and one of the things that I proudly told all those present, was that my father planted short crops and provisions for consumption by our family of seven. This helped to significantly supplement his public servant's salary, which was the main source of income in our family, since my mother was a 'stay-at-home' mom. My Mom did contribute financially also by making cakes, wines, cheese straws and other things to sell.

As my savings dwindled, I naturally turned to some do-it-yourself gardening, making more use of local produce which grew in my land and buying more local produce from our national produce company, which buys from local farmers in bulk and then sells to retail consumers like me.

Always try, as best as possible, to buy organically grown food products or those with as little chemical input as possible. The latter may be your best bet, though, since not many farmers use purely organic means of growing their produce. The reason for this declining use of purely organic crop production is that farmers want greater crop yield, reduced incidences of pest infestation and the ability to produce and harvest crops outside of their traditional harvesting seasons.

If you buy imported produce, as opposed to locally grown produce, you increase the likelihood of being exposed to even more chemicals in your food, since preservatives will be used in order to slow down the ripening process during transportation and to keep the produce fresh. So buy local!

If you're new to planting your own produce and you have little or no land around you to do planting, then you can practice container gardening. There are lots of online container gardening tutorials, via YouTube, that can show you how to creatively plant food in literally any small space.

You can also review my article titled '1 Essential Pair of Garden Tools with Gardening Tips' for some useful gardening tips that I have employed myself. You'll be given step-by-step instructions, with accompanying useful photos, on how to successfully begin doing your own gardening; from planting the seeds in your tiny nursery to proudly harvesting your own vegetables. (Read it at http://heidivincent.hubpages.com/hub/1-essential-pair-of-garden-tools-with-gardening-tips)

I also share with you some little know information about companion gardening, that is, things that you should and should not plant next to each other.

What YOU Can Do! – Get Started on Survivor Strategy No. 2

Apply the principle of growing what you eat, eating what you grow and buying local. Here's what I did and what you can do too:

1. Grow some vegetables and seasonings for yourself *(At various points, I grew Chive, Thyme, Rosemary, Seasoning Peppers, Sweet Peppers, Pigeon Peas, Plantain, Green Fig, and experimented with Tomatoes, Carrots & Cucumbers).*

2. Buy local produce - fruits, vegetables and provision - from your local produce store or a farmer's market *(Food always costs a lot less at a local produce store or a farmer's market, as opposed to a supermarket, and its healthier too).*

3. Always steam your vegetables and provisions instead of boiling them *(More nutrients are preserved when food is steamed. See my article titled '**The Best Food Steamer - An Oster of Course!**'* at http://heidivincent.hubpages.com/hub/the-best-oster-food-steamer *for more benefits of steaming your food).*

May all that you plant bear plenty!

Survivor Strategy 3
Going Meatless Isn't All That Bad!

> *"There is no doubt that some plant food, such as oatmeal, is more economical than meat, and superior to it in regard to both mechanical and mental performance. Such food, moreover, taxes our digestive organs decidedly less, and, in making us more contented and sociable, produces an amount of good difficult to estimate."* ~ *Nikola Tesla*

I stopped eating meat in 1998, long before I became unemployed in 2010. So my reasons for stopping eat meat were not related to unemployment but it turned out to be an extremely advantageous move, with tremendous benefits during my period of unemployment.

I actually stopped eating meat, temporarily, at the suggestion of an herbalist, in order to figure out the cause of a pimple breakout on my face at age 27. It turned out that my meat consumption was not the cause of my pimple breakout but I felt so good for the few weeks that I had temporarily stopped eating meat that I stopped eating meat for good, permanently.

So to date, I am a Pesca-Ovo Vegetarian (Pesco-Vegetarian), which means that I don't eat meat but I do eat fish, milk, eggs and egg-based foods, such as mayonnaise, unlike a vegan (strict vegetarian).

You will not believe the amount of savings you will make from eliminating meat from your diet plus the fact that you will be experiencing a healthier you. I am proof of it!

Although, like I said earlier, I could still eat fish, there were many times that I just could not even afford fish. So I supplemented my diet with lots of beans and peas in order to get my recommended daily allowance (RDA) of protein.

On better days, I bought salt-fish *(also known as salted cod or bacalao)* and chipped up (shredded) small pieces of saltfish to add to soup, rice, fish cakes and salads or I used it with lots of shredded vegetables, onions and sweet peppers.

What YOU Can Do! – Get Started on Survivor Strategy No. 3

Apply the principle of cutting meat from your diet. Here's what I did and what you can do too:

1. Use dried peas and soak overnight before cooking *(Canned peas and beans are a lot more expensive)*.

2. Use salt-fish instead of meat *(salt fish is very versatile and you can shred it really small and mix with shredded vegetables like carrots and cabbage*

in order to increase its yield and stretch it over several meals).

3. Use fish instead of meat *(chicken, pork, beef, lamb, etcetera).* When using fish, cut it up in small nugget sizes and season it before frying it in a mixture of flour, baking powder and water. Then make a ketchup sauce and place the fried fish pieces in the ketchup sauce *(With this cooking tip, you can add a little more body to the fish pieces giving the illusion of having bigger pieces of fish and it will allow you to stretch the fish over several meals).*

Note Well: After frying the fish nuggets, you can refrigerate or freeze them. Only place them in the ketchup sauce on the day that you plan to use them in a meal.

May all of the foods that you eat, from the earth and sea, bring you all of the essential nutrients that your body requires!

Survivor Strategy 4
Do Your Own Cooking

"Cooking is like painting or writing a song. Just as there are only so many notes or colors, there are only so many flavors - it's how you combine them that sets you apart." ~ *Wolfgang Puck*

I like cooking but I won't say that I love cooking so much as to become a great chef. However, as anyone who has tasted my food will tell you, I am a pretty good cook.

I have to seriously thank my Mom for teaching me to cook at an early age - somewhere around 9 or 10 years - and for her wonderful cooking skills. By age 13, she delegated the cooking of Sunday meals to my sister and I. So, every other Sunday, one of us was responsible for cooking the entire Sunday meal.

Sunday meals at our home were always an extravagant affair, with varied types of dishes. At first, because of the number of dishes we cooked, in keeping with the way my Mom prepared Sunday meals, we served meals extremely late - between 3 to 4 p.m. - as we tried to master our varied dishes. With time and practice, over the years, however, meal preparation time was significantly reduced.

If you're new to cooking, you will find yourself obsessed with specific measurements for ingredients as you try to get the recipe just right. This normally adds to your meal preparation time. However, over time you will be able to approximate ingredient measures, which will help to reduce your cooking time.

Now if I think I can cook, wait until my mother cooked for you. My Mom had a hand and eye for food. She always just knew how to combine the right colours and tastes to make a finger licking, good meal. She didn't attend any kind of cooking classes, have any cookbooks or have access to the internet for recipes. It was just one of her God-given talents.

She loved to entertain guests, when we were growing up, and everyone who ate her meals, without exception, would sing her high praises for whatever meal she prepared.

There are three key reasons, however, why I almost always cook my own food and why I would advocate this to any and every one:

1. You will save a significant amount of money *(If you don't believe me, then do this simple test; make note of the ingredients of your next*

purchased meal and get the price of the raw ingredients).

2. You have control over portions *(Food is often sold in portions that are too large. Most times, the portions tend to be more than we would normally eat and if, like me, you hate to waste or throw away food, then you force to eat it all. This leads to over eating over time and consequent weight gain).*

3. You have control over the amount of sugar, salt and preservatives in your food *(Restaurants cook primarily for taste. If that means throwing in a 'boat load' of sugar, salt or preservatives, then that's precisely what they will do without regard to what's healthy for you. When you cook for yourself, you can limit the amount of salt, sugar or seasonings to what's healthy for you, especially if you already suffer with diabetes &/or hypertension).*

If you're not a first class cook like my Mom, or a first class runner-up cook like me, there's no need to despair. We all had to start from scratch, with terrible meals that were not even fit for the dogs. With time, experimentation and persistence, anyone, including you, can become a good cook.

Free Cooking Recipes

Here are a few of my recipes that are online favourites with readers:

1. Mango Almond Cupcake and Cake Recipe
   http://heidivincent.hubpages.com/hub/mango-almond-cupcake-and-cake-recipe

2. How to Make a Really Good Caribbean Fish Broth - Fish Soup   http://food.squidoo.com/how-to-make-a-really-good-caribbean-fish-broth-fish-soup

3. Cheesy Vegetable & Macaroni Pie
   http://heidivincent.hubpages.com/hub/cheesy-vegetable-macaroni-pie

4. Lip Smacking Good Steamed Ground Provisions and Vegetables with Saltfish
   http://heidivincent.hubpages.com/hub/lip-smacking-good-steamed-ground-provisions-and-vegetables-with-saltfish

5. Delicious Spaghetti Recipe with Tuna Sauce, Juicy Tomatoes and Cheese
   http://heidivincent.hubpages.com/hub/delicious-spaghetti-recipe-with-tuna-sauce-juicy-tomatoes-and-cheese

Apply the principle of cooking your own meals. Here's what I did and what you can do too:

1. Look at online videos for visual help with preparing some of your favourite meals, especially if you are new to cooking.

2. Search for online recipes for the ingredients that you have or are able to afford *(This is especially useful if you have limited ingredients or are looking for new ways of preparing traditional foods)*.

3. When planning your meals always think of adding as much **colour** and **nutrition** as possible *(Green foods are good for detoxifying your body; red foods are good for blood and keeping your heart strong; yellow foods are good for your joints; purple foods are associated with giving you long life – longevity. The varied colours also make food attractive to look at)*.

4. Add a clove of raw, grated garlic to your salads to give them a wonderful flavor, lower your blood pressure and fight against any oncoming illnesses caused by viruses.

5. Avoid mindless eating *(You are likely to eat more when you eat while working or watching television*

23

with the unfavourable outcome over time of weight gain).

6. Use ketchup to make sauces *(Place quarter cup of water, 2 tablespoons of ketchup, a tinge of cooking butter, a few slices of onion and some chopped chive in a saucepan and cook for 2 to 3 minutes to produce a thick and tasty sauce).*

7. Tweak original recipes to your taste by adding more or less of ingredients *(Just because the recipe says 3 cups of coconut does not mean you have to use 3 cups of coconut if you do not particularly like coconut. I always try new recipes the first time exactly as it is given in the recipe. Then once I taste it, I make adjustments, thereafter, to complement my own taste by adding, reducing or taking out certain ingredients).*

8. Bake your own bread *(Use half portion of whole wheat flour and half portion of white flour to bake healthy bread with lots of fibre. You can bake for 3-4 weeks at a time and freeze the bread that you will not be using in the current week, in order to preserve its freshness. Place the bread in foil paper and then put it in a plastic bag to avoid it getting wet in the freezer. When you are ready to use the frozen bread, take it out of the freezer and place it in a non-freezing section of the fridge to thaw out and then you can take it out of the*

refrigerator the next day and place it on the counter top to finish thawing out. Use it at room temperature or toast it to your desired crispiness).

May the food that you prepare provide nutrition and give delight, in both sight and taste, to all who consume it!

Survivor Strategy 5
Learn New Skills &/or Improve Your Existing Skills

"I keep 6 honest serving-men: They taught me all I know. Their names are What and Where and When and How and Why and Who." ~ Rudyard Kipling

One of the things I really love about myself is that I am a continuous learner. Being a continuous learner is a very useful quality, especially when you're unemployed and looking to find new employment or income earning opportunities.

You can learn more about an area that you already know about or you can branch out into learning some new things and expand your existing skills set.

You can also take up or start back doing a craft that you learnt, such as crocheting, painting, wood carving, cooking…and the list goes on. I have a friend who crochets/knits baby clothes for pay. I also know an old school mate of mine who cooks from his home for a living. He does not have a restaurant but he takes daily food orders from people at different work places and delivers the food to them. So he avoids any kind of overheads that a restaurant owner will have by cooking from his own home.

The good news is that there are lots of free online courses on just about anything you want to know more about on the internet. For example, as I started to write online for pay and set up my Catholic Contributor website - http://www.thecatholiccontributor.com - I realized that I needed to improve my social media and html skills. For me, W3Schools.com and Massive Open Online Courses (MOOC) proved very useful.

What YOU Can Do! – Get Started on Survivor Strategy No. 5

Apply the principle of improving and expanding your skills set. Here's what I did and what you can do too:

1. Search for and do free online or face-to-face courses. *(This can be in an area that you already know a lot about, an area that you always wanted to know more about or a new area to supplement a completely new path that you have taken or are hoping to take).*

2. Learn a new skill that is completely different from your job qualification, especially if you are a professional. *(Choosing something that you love or are very passionate about will sustain you even if things stay tough financially for a while).*

May God make you a good steward of the gifts and talents he has blessed you with and the new skills that you will learn!

Survivor Strategy 6

Find Other Cheap Sources of Entertainment besides Cable Television

> *"Since I have access to every, every crisis in the world because it's always blaring at me on cable television, that doesn't mean I have to worry about every one of them. This is also known as knowing where the off button is" ~ Eric Schmidt*

On January 21, I calmly called the cable company and told them to disconnect my cable service with **immediate effect**! The only person who seemed to be panicking was the Service Delivery Manager, who was trying her best to convince me not to cut the service so abruptly.

I calmly explained to her that I was unemployed, that I did not want to incur further debt and that I would be following up my telephone conversation to her with an official letter, which I sent via email later that very said day. My telling her that I was unemployed did not cause her to waver in her bids to get me to keep the cable service connected, at least until the end of the month.

Cutting my cable television service was like going back to basics for me but I also reminded myself that it was not a bad move for the following reasons:

1. I had done it twice before, when I was studying for my first degree and my master's degree, and I had survived.

2. I would be saving $60 each month that I could put to better use by meeting my increasingly late utility bill payments *(That was $720 in one year!!! To an unemployed person like me, at that point, that was A LOT of money!)*

3. There was little that really interested me on cable television, anyway. When I had cable television, my television consumption basically consisted of local nightly news, BBC News, 'Dancing with the Stars' and comedy re-runs, like Cosby and Friends, during the week, and Sunday evening movies on PBS. Otherwise, there was nothing worth watching on cable television. So it was no loss really, when I look at it retrospectively.

4. It gave me the opportunity to channel those idle moments into online writing in order to generate some income, however little.

When I was employed, I had both cable television and internet service. I paid $60 for cable television and $69 for unlimited internet service and I did not maximize my use of either service. I was scarcely using the internet at home, since I had access to the internet at work. However, I also wanted the convenience of being able to log on to the internet, at home, without having to pay extra for running over my time limit on a limited internet service plan.

When I turned off my cable television service, during my unemployment period, I was able to consolidate my entertainment expenses and actually make better use of my $69 unlimited internet package, while diverting the $60 that I previously spent on cable television each month toward more urgent living expenses.

So I would advise you to switch to an unlimited internet service package instead of a pay per usage package, since you will now be making a lot more use of your internet service, if you follow my advice. It works out cheaper overall.

What YOU Can Do! – Get Started on Survivor Strategy No. 6

Apply the principle of finding good and cheap entertainment outside of cable television. Here's what I did and what you can do too:

1. Watch old movies, especially classics, online on YouTube *(Newly released movies are usually blocked online and some of the other websites that they can be seen on are usually dangerous sites*

that can place viruses and spyware on your computer).

2. Play online games, such as Scrabble. *(There are options to play against one or more computers or with real live persons online who are searching for good, clean entertainment like you).*

3. Download and install offline game apps, such as Word Press, Word Search and Sudoku, on your phone *(This is especially useful if you do not have internet connection at all or have limited access to internet connection).*

4. Listen to online radio or listen to music online *(There are numerous playlists for all kinds of music genres. So you can literally click on one of them and have song after song play while you relax and work or search online).*

5. Skype with friends *(This has saved me countless dollars in overseas calls and I could still stay connected while seeing and hearing my friends who lived abroad).*

6. Mingle and keep abreast of what's happening in the world and with friends on Facebook *(When I was unemployed, I actually had no time for Facebook. However, during my period of unemployment, because I spent most of my time at home and did not have to leave home, Facebook helped to keep me abreast of what was happening).*

May God bless you with hobbies that will renew you mentally, physically and spiritually and may He make you a blessing to those with whom you socialize!

Survivor Strategy 7
Continuously Praise, Worship and Thank God!!!

> *"Amen! Praise, glory, wisdom, thanksgiving, honor, power, and might belong to our God forever and ever! Amen!" ~ Revelation 7:12*

When we're experiencing difficulties and challenges in life, especially if they're over a long period of time, we eventually develop tunnel vision that causes us to focus too closely and exclusively on our situation.

I think this may have been the case with me, until, one Sunday in May, while reading Nancy Leigh DeMoss' book titled *'A Place of Quiet Rest'*, I took hold of a brilliant idea of hers in the book. One of the ways that she suggested one could make her/his praise to God personal was to "Write your own psalm of praise, thanking God for His character, for His works on your behalf, and for physical and spiritual blessings you have received from Him."

I immediately went to work on her suggestion and on that Sunday in May, having been already unemployed for three long years, I wrote **'My Personal Psalm of Praise and Thanksgiving to God'**.

As I took pen and paper in hand, and began to write about all the things that I was thankful to God about, I was surprised for two main reasons:

1. All of the things that I wanted to praise and thank God for just flowed from my mind to my hand effortlessly as I began to write.

2. I could not believe all of the things that God had done for me and that I was taking for granted because I was obsessed with that one area of my life that was not going well and causing it to steal all of my joy.

Since there are 150 Psalms in the Holy Bible, I affectionately dubbed it **my Psalm 151** and this is how it reads:

I praise, thank, glorify and honour you God!
For your constant love and protection!
For always being here for me!
For guiding my steps and actions!
For giving me the necessary solutions to problems and challenges!
For keeping me safe from harm!
For giving me that inner peace that surpasseth all understanding!

Thank you for blessing me with good health and keeping debilitating and death threatening diseases and illnesses from me!

Thank you for the continuous wisdom and knowledge you give me to care for my physical, spiritual, mental and emotional well-being!

Thank you for showing me mercy and forgiving my sins of disobedience!

I praise you God for being you!

I praise and thank you God for your daily interventions in my life that, in retrospect, affirm to me that your timing is indeed perfect!

I praise and thank you God for the special gift of loving and caring friends that you have given me!

I praise and thank you God for giving me that continuous comforting feeling of your omniscient, omnipotent and omnipresent presence in every area and circumstance of my life!

I praise and thank you God for the wisdom, knowledge, understanding, and commonsense that you have given me in worldly and spiritual matters!

Thank you God! Thank you God! Thank you God!

To you, O God, be highest glory, honour and praise!

Amen! Alleluia! Thank you God!
[by Heidi E. Vincent]

One of my favourite praise Psalms in the Bible is **Psalm 34**. In particular, I like the very first three verses, where the psalmist proclaims:

"I will always thank the Lord;
I will never stop praising him.
I will praise him for what he has done;
may all who are oppressed listen and be glad!
Proclaim with me the Lord's greatness;
let us praise his name together!"

What it so powerfully encourages us to do, is to praise God in all seasons of our life, including when things are not so great with us, when we are unemployed and when we are burdened by financial worries.

So whatever, difficult situation you're facing right now or will face in the future, always remember to give God continuous praise. Giving praise, especially in difficult circumstances, is one of the ways that you can help yourself to get a breakthrough in your situation. Just like Paul and Silas were delivered from prison after singing hymns of praise *(Acts 16)*, you will receive deliverance from your unemployment and/or financial situation.

What YOU Can Do! – Get Started on Survivor Strategy No. 7

Apply the principle of continuously praising, worshiping and thanking God. Here's what I did and what you can do too:

1. Write your very own 'Praise & Thanksgiving Psalm' to God *(If you need a little help with starting your own, you can read about my process for creating my own in my article titled '**How to Create Your Own Psalm like King David**' at http://heidivincent.hubpages.com/hub/how-to-create-your-own-psalm-like-king-david)*.

2. Read one of the 150 Psalms in the Bible each day *(This serves to develop a continuous spirit of worship, praise and thanksgiving in you)*.

3. Start your day by thanking God for ordinary things such as, keeping you safe during the night, awakening you to see another day, for breath, health, food to eat, a warm bed to sleep in, and whatever else you would like to thank him for.

4. Conclude your day by reflecting on the things that occurred during the day and thanking God for specific things or situations that happened in your favour.

5. Start the healthy habit of thanking everyone who does something for you, whether it is a big or small favour, and praying for them.

6. Begin each of your lengthy prayer sessions with a few joyful, worship choruses, hymns or religious songs *(This always proves to be a great mood setter. No matter how 'low' or depressed you are feeling, once you begin to sing, your spirit will be lifted. It is especially important to do this 5-7 minute worship singing session when you do not feel like doing it. Starting will take great effort on your part, when things are at their worst and you do not feel to sing at all, but once you get into the first 3-4 minutes, you will always experience a positive change in your mood.)*

May you never forget or take for granted God's goodness to you and may praise issue forth continuously to Him from your mouth!

Survivor Strategy 8
Use Prayer, Music, Meditation & Affirmations to Keep Your Spirits High

Depression does kill!!! When you face ongoing unemployment that stretches over months or, even worse, years and bills keep piling up, a natural offshoot is depression because you feel helpless about your situation, especially when you can see no end to your problems in sight.

Honestly, there were days when I went to bed asking God to take my life as I slept. I wanted to 'wake up dead' – if you know what I mean. I cannot ever remember wanting to die so desperately in my life before. In those moments, I was also deeply empathetic with persons who had committed suicide. In fact, as often as I prayed away the spirit of suicide in my life, I prayed for all those who had committed suicide because in my present situation I could clearly see how they had arrived at that point.

As a Catholic Christian, I believe in the Catholic Church doctrines which teach, that, **"We should not despair of the eternal salvation of persons who have taken their own lives. By ways known to him alone, God can provide the opportunity for salutary repentance. The Church prays for persons who have taken their own**

lives" *(Catechism of the Catholic Church; paragraphs 2280 – 2283)*

Nonetheless, I constantly told myself that suicide was not an option for me because I thought about how I would be offending God by taking my own life, as well as how I would be throwing away all of the supportive efforts of my wonderful friends who had done their very best to keep me going financially.

A powerful combination of praying, listening to uplifting music, doing spiritual meditation and using daily affirmations is what I used to keep from falling into depression or staying depressed, whenever I became too overwhelmed by my unemployment and financial problems now and then.

I urge you to fervently use this powerful, 4-pronged, combination strategy of prayer, music, meditation and affirmation, like I did, in order to keep depression at bay. None of the strategies is any good by itself; so use them simultaneously.

The Prayer Factor

"We have to pray with our eyes on God, not on the difficulties." ~ Oswald Chambers.

"Prayer breaks all bars, dissolves all chains, opens all prisons, and widens all straits by which God's saints have been held." ~ E. M. Bounds

I prayed all through the day but I had two lengthy prayer periods in particular; first thing in the morning and on evenings or late at night. Those lengthier prayer sessions lasted for at least one hour and were more structured.

My Morning Prayer period followed the form of the Lord's Prayer (Our Father) - *Praise, Petition, Confession, Thanksgiving* - which Jesus taught the disciples when they asked Him to teach them how to pray *(Matthew 6:9-13 & Luke 11:1-4).*

I would begin by praising God with hymns or spiritual songs. I would follow this with some reflective readings from a daily devotional, such as 'Living Faith', 'Our Daily Bread' or 'The Good Seed'. Then I would read a few scripture verses from the Holy Bible and say my 'Living Rosary'. Next, I would bring my unemployment and financial situations before God and ask Him to provide for me and help me with those problems and all of my other resultant problems.

Finally, I would speak to Him about the ill feelings that I was harbouring against those who had betrayed me and done me harm and the anger I felt towards my family and the false friends I had purged myself of. I would ask Him to keep me from becoming a bitter person as a result of my current difficulties and then I would conclude with the relevant morning prayers from the 'Psalter of the Divine Office'.

Now it is important for me to let you know that since I could not afford to buy the quarterly devotional booklets from 'Living Faith' or 'Our Daily Bread', while I was unemployed, I recycled the old ones that I had bought in previous years when I was working. So for example, I can clearly remember that for the 3-month period from July to September in 2015, I used the 2009 'Living Faith' devotional booklet for the same period from July to September in 2015.

My prayers during the day were mainly one sentence utterances, such as 'Thank you, God!', 'Jesus, please help me', 'Dear God, please order my steps today', 'Dear God, please help me to be a blessing to each and every person whom I encounter today', and such like.

My Afternoon/Night Prayer period involved saying one mystery of the Holy Rosary - Joyful, Sorrowful, Glorious or Luminous - followed by listening to a really cool, no AMAZING, Catholic app called 'Laudate' (*you can download it for free on Google Play* https://play.google.com/store/apps/details?id=com.aycka. apps.MassReadings)

There is a tonne load of really good material there. I focused on the very first link when you open the app, titled 'Daily Readings, Saint of the Day'. On entering that section, I usually listened to the podcasts of the daily scripture readings and three different and spiritually provocative daily meditations from Regnum Christi, Pope Emeritus Benedict XVI and pray-as-you-go. I would then read the stimulating 'Reflections' and conclude with the very informative reading on the 'Saint of the Day'.

I cannot explain to you how much I looked forward to those two lengthy prayer sessions, in particular, and how they helped to refresh, nourish and sustain me spiritually, mentally and emotionally each day.

There were days when I honestly did not feel like doing anything, including praying, but I prayed anyway and so should you.

> *"Don't pray when you feel like it. Have an appointment with the Lord and keep it. A man is powerful on his knees." ~ Corrie ten Boom*

The Music Factor

"Music washes away from the soul the dust of everyday life." ~ Berthold Auerbach

There's something magically wonderful, powerful and empowering about music! As a Negro woman and the descendant of slaves, who were brought by force from Africa to the Caribbean on slave ships, music, singing and dancing is in my blood. I can well understand and relate to how singing sustained the spirits of my ancestors during the darkest period of their lives – slavery.

As a Christian, through praising God with music and song, I have also experienced the same liberation from difficult situations as Paul and Silas experienced when they were praising God while bound in prison and were miraculously released from their shackles, had the doors to the prison opened and received news that the Roman authorities had ordered their release from prison *(Acts 16:20-36)*. In short, listening to good uplifting music and singing yourself, whether or not you have a great singing voice, during your period of unemployment and financial stress, is another powerful way to keep depression at bay and sustain your spirit.

I sing or listen to gospel music when I need to lift my spirits and praise God. I sing or listen to classical music when I need to soothe my spirit or concentrate. I sing or listen to calypso, soca, reggae and Latin music when I want to celebrate or bring some joy to my life when things are going really badly.

You can listen to some of the various genres of music that I listen to in my article titled '**My Music: All Time Favorite Soundtracks**' at http://heidivincent.hubpages.com/hub/my-music-all-time-favorite-soundtracks and on my Christian website at http://www.thecatholiccontributor.com/music.html

Your choice of music may be completely different from mine and that's perfectly alright. Just learn which type of music does what for you and how it affects you. Then just listen to what your spirit needs in each moment and play that genre of music.

The Meditation Factor

> *"If I had not been already meditating, I would certainly have had to start. I've treated my own depression for many years with exercise and meditation, and I've found that to be a tremendous help." ~ Judy Collins*

I strongly believe in alternative medicine and consider myself a spiritual person, as opposed to a religious person. So for my own well-being, I had been using herbal medicine, meditation, chakra healing, and things like that, in order to maintain my well-being long before I became unemployed.

49

During unemployment, all of these, plus the things that I have mentioned in this chapter, helped to keep me spiritually centered, focused and with few bouts of depression. So, **meditation is the next powerful recovery tool that I will be telling you about next.**

When I was growing up, we had a ceramic plaque on the living room wall of our home which had a quote by Erma Bombeck written on it and which read as follows, *"Worry is like a rocking chair: it gives you something to do but never gets you anywhere"*. There was a little old lady in a rocking chair painted next to the words on it and if you think of it, just like you pretty much remain in position while rocking away, no matter how hard, no matter how much you worry about your problems, they will not go anywhere. You have to get up and do something about them.

Now it is natural to find yourself worrying. After all, who can be unemployed and be experiencing financial distress without worrying? I worried a lot during my unemployment period but I used meditation as one of the outlets for my worry.

In particular, I participated in the free **Oprah & Deepak 21-day Meditation** experiences that were gifted to persons online, approximately every four months.

Oprah Winfrey is a renowned media owner and popular talk show host who partnered with Deepak Chopra, a well-known, Indian-born, physician who practices alternative medicine and is a strong advocate of spiritual meditation.

In combination with the other things that I have outlined in this chapter - *prayer, music and affirmations* - meditation really helped me to refocus my energy away from my problems and expand my mind to embrace other positive things in my life, such as:

a. My perfect physical health.

b. The wonderful gifts and talents that God has blessed me with, such as writing, a very analytical mind and an spirit of encouragement.

c. The spirit of discernment, which often enabled me to recognize people's true intentions.

d. Great friends who I have shared many wonderful moments and experiences with, when I was employed, and who loved and supported me through my season of unemployment.

How meditation helped me, and will definitely help you as well, is that whenever I began to worry, I would refocus that negative energy towards doing one or more of the concrete things that I have outlined in this book, in order to pull myself out of depression and my situation.

Meditation doesn't have to be a formal process either like the Oprah & Deepak meditation sessions. It can simply involve you doing something that you love, such as listening to music, fishing, playing tennis or scrabble, socializing with friends; whatever takes you to a joyful and/or peaceful place.

As Deepak Chopra explains, in his website article titled **'Holding Focus - Why You Need This Awareness Skill'**, *"...apply your focus to the things that charm you. Put your energy on things you love but also on things that most easily hold your attention and make you feel energized and vital"*.

The Affirmation Factor

> *"Affirmations are statements going beyond the reality of the present into the creation of the future through the words you use in the now."* ~ Louise L. Hay

An affirmation is a sort of pronouncement, declaration or positive statement that you or someone else makes about a situation. Affirming your own self, as well as the things and situations in your life is an excellent and totally legitimate kind of self-love.

In fact, part of meditation, which we looked at early, involves the use of affirmations.

You can create your own affirmations or search the internet for a plethora of existing affirmations in whatever area of your life that you are experiencing challenges and want to experience an improvement or change for the better.

Affirmations are often very simple and encompass, in the specific wording, validation of a positive outcome that you want in a particular area. For example, with respect to your deteriorating finances and ongoing unemployment situation, you can use any of the 100 popular affirmations from Prolific Life, such as:

a. *"Money comes to me easily and effortlessly"*.

b. *"My thoughts are my reality so I think up a bright new day."*

c. *"All that I need comes to me at the right time and place in this life."*

d. *"I refuse to give up because I haven't tried all possible ways."*

e. *"I am a money magnet and attract wealth and abundance."*

f. *"All my problems have a solution."*

g. *"Everything works out for my highest good."*

I have used numerous affirmations over the five plus years that I have been unemployed but there were two in particular that I wrote out and pasted onto my bathroom/toilet door, as constant reminders:

"A Quitter Never Wins and a Winner Never Quits!"
and
"Temporary Defeat is not Permanent Failure!"

Then one day, I had an epiphany!!! A really bright light bulb went on in my head! It's amazing how you can know about something and not be doing it or doing it well. I knew about affirmations for a long while and I knew the process really well. But then one day, while talking about affirmations, I suddenly realized that I myself was not fully utilizing this powerful tool in my own life. So then, I also wrote out and posted the following three affirmations near my computer, where I spent almost the whole day and night, and on my bathroom mirror:

"Everything works out for my highest good!"
and
"Money comes to me easily and effortlessly!"
and

"All that I need comes to me at the right time and place in my life!"

How had I not thought about this before? I was awestruck to say the least!

Now, once you have chosen the affirmations that you want, you have to follow up with **the MOST IMPORTANT part – saying them often and with a believing heart!**

When someone gives you a genuine smile, you can feel it. Likewise, when someone gives you a fake smile you can feel it too; something about it just doesn't sit right with you even though you may be seeing all of their teeth and their dimples too, if they have. There is always a missing 'light' in their eyes, which reflects the real mood and intentions of their heart and soul.

Well, the same is true with the use of affirmations. You cannot lie to your heart and spirit. If you're just saying the words without believing them, your heart and spirit will know this and you will not experience improvement in your circumstances.

One of my very first and all-time favourite affirmations, which I still love very much, over and above all the rest, is as follows:

"God is my Provider! Whatever my needs are, they are met speedily and in Divine Order. I am thankful for this awareness. God is my Provider! "

The main problem, though, was that I was not saying it as often as I should have been saying it. I believed it with all of my heart but I only started saying it more often after my epiphany.

So don't be like me. I am equipping you with all of the information you need to know about the process of affirmation and I urge you to start looking for or creating your very own affirmations, today, about what you want to change in your life.

Finally, the last, but by no means least ingredient when using affirmations is that you have to be **persistent.** In other words, you can't say the affirmations for a week or a month and then stop if you aren't seeing physical signs of your situation changing. You have to keep on saying the affirmations until your physical situation or circumstances change, no matter how long it takes. That's a synopsis of what we Christians describe as 'faith'. You have to believe it before you see it. Not the other way around.

Apply the principle of fighting depression, anxiety and worry with prayers, music, meditation and affirmations. Here's what I did and what you can do too:

1. Pray, read your Bible and use inspirational readings daily *(Praying often serves to give you direction and reading the Bible often provides encouragement and strengthens you spiritually and emotionally)*.

2. Sing and listen to uplifting music *(Good music always lifts the spirit, as numerous research has shown; such a simple yet powerful tool)*.

3. Create your own playlist on your computer to listen to when you are offline *(You can find free music in whatever genres you like online)*.

4. Use the AM/FM radio on your phone to listen to music.

5. Get a small, battery operated AM/FM radio *(One of my Aunts gave me one)*.

6. Search for and use good, free online meditations, such as the Oprah & Deepak 21-day meditation experiences. *(These meditation experiences will open your eyes to see beyond your current unemployment and financial struggles and release*

you temporarily from the albatross of your current challenges).

7. Write and place affirmations at strategic points in your home and repeat them to yourself often with a believing heart *(Since the bathroom/toilet was a place that I frequented throughout the day, I had 5 key affirmations posted on my bathroom/toilet door as constant reminders. Any place that you spend a lot of time is a good place to put up such affirmations).*

8. Pray continuously against the spirit of suicide *(With no sight of an end to your unemployment and financial woes, this may seem as an easy way out but if you press on, no matter how difficult it is right now, you will one day live to be able to look back on this 'valley' period and be thankful that you did not quit at that point).*

May your mind, spirit and emotions be renewed when you pray and meditate!

Survivor Strategy 9
Exercise Daily

"To enjoy the glow of good health, you must exercise. ~ Gene Tunney

While I was unemployed, walking proved to be my best exercise, from both a physical standpoint and a mental perspective. Physically, I was able to keep my legs and heart strong, by being forced to take a half mile trek to the main road when my vehicle was repossessed. Mentally, I was able to use the time to pray, mull over solutions to various challenges and clear my head. So I have to say that I wholeheartedly agree with Thomas Jefferson, who stated that, *"Walking is the best possible exercise. Habituate yourself to walk very far."*

Over the years, including during my unemployment period, I have also used various floor exercises to successfully keep in shape. Those floor exercises only require a floor mat and an optional exercise ball. In fact, so successful is my home exercise routine, that one of the comments that former classmates, who I have not seen in many years, often make is that I look the same as when I was in school. My exercise routine plus eating healthy is what I credit for being able to maintain my ideal weight. I have shared the link to one of my routines with you, below.

Of course, there are lots of great exercise routines online that you can adopt or you can create your own exercise routine, like I did, using a combination of exercises that work for you. Whether you adopt an existing exercise routine as your own or create your very own mix-and-match exercise routine, make sure that it includes all of the following elements:

1. Warm up exercises *(Whether you are just starting back to exercise, after failing to exercise in ages, or you are accustomed exercising, this is a very important part of your exercise routine that will help you avoid getting pain from strained or sprained muscles. Warm up exercises put your body on alert that you will be engaging it in heavy workout activity shortly)*.

2. Exercises that target your abdominals and obliques *(As we age, it becomes increasingly difficult to maintain a flat stomach without some form of disciplined exercise routine that specifically targets those muscles)*.

3. Exercises that tone the muscles in your arms, legs and buttocks *(As part of the aging process, skin losses its elasticity, the results of which are wrinkles and sagging muscles. This part of the aging process can be significantly slowed down, if one engages in regular exercise to tone these muscles and keep them firm)*.

4. Cool down exercises *(These provide a calming transition from the hectic workout back to your regular activities)*.

5. Drink the recommended 6 to 8 glasses of water daily, so that your body can remain hydrated and cleanse itself. You will also have less hunger pangs *(A surprisingly unknown fact is that dehydrated persons tend to eat more. Many people, not realizing that their bodies are calling for water, eat more food or snacks in an attempt to fill the seeming hunger pangs that they experience)*.

What YOU Can Do! – Get Started on Survivor Strategy No. 9

Apply the principle of exercising daily and drinking water regularly. Here's what I did and what you can do too:

1. Walk for at least 30 minutes, 3 times a week, at a brisk pace *(This increases your heart rate and will help you to keep excess weight off, thereby maintaining your ideal weight, if you are currently at your ideal weight)*.

2. Do some effective floor exercises, at least 3 times per week, that will target your abdominal muscles, since this is one of the very first places where

people experience fat buildup *(This is a cheap but very effective strategy, as opposed to paying expensive gym fees to do workouts with fancy equipment.*

*You can see one of my exercise routines that I have been successfully doing for years in my article titled '**How to Get Fit and Keep Fit With 12 Home Exercises**'* at *http://heidivincent.hubpages.com/hub/how-to-get-fit-and-keep-fit-with-12-home-exercises)*.

3. Search online for free and effective home exercise routines.

May God drive far from you all debilitating, death threatening and painful diseases and illnesses!

Survivor Strategy 10

Don't Let Pride Keep You from Reaching Out For Help

"Until we can receive with an open heart, we're never really giving with an open heart. When we attach judgment to receiving help, we knowingly or unknowingly attach judgment to giving help." ~ Brené Brown

After crying my eyes out in despair, for a whole night, over the realization that I would have to reach out for major financial help, I contacted some friends and one family member explaining my true situation.

I'll be frank about it! **No help came from any of my family members.** However, **I had 4 friends who immediately reached out and helped** in such significant ways that, I pray God will tremendously bless their lives. Two other friends responded some time later. My immediate neighbours were a real blessing in my life. I pray God's continuous blessing on that family!

Now let me tell you about some of God's awesomeness and the love of my friends in the middle of my financial crisis and ongoing unemployment situation. I remember being extremely grateful and truly loved but also feeling a bit embarrassed that I had to be helped like this.

When I telephoned one particular friend in another country, she told me that earlier in the week she and her husband had discussed my unemployment situation and they had decided to send me some money. Then she went on to tell me that as her husband left their home that very morning, the last thing he had said to her was "Don't forget to fix up that thing *(meaning the money)* for Heidi." She also told me that given my current situation that she was hearing, they would send me more than they had decided to send previously. **All of it was a gift; not a loan!**

My heart soared with gratitude and I marveled at the awesomeness of God who had placed it on their hearts to reach out and help me even before I made that desperate phone call.

On another occasion, these same friends sent me 3 boxes crammed with groceries from another country and, unknowingly, saved me from having my electricity cut during one Christmas season, when the wife sent me a Christmas present of cash through a colleague of hers who was attending a conference in my country.

Another friend who had responded earlier to my financial plea with a very generous loan, also gave me the startup funds for my coffee business, with me still owing her the original amount that she had loaned me.

When I couldn't even buy coffee products to sell, after waiting for a whole half year to get some kind of job, another 2 friends gave me the money to buy some coffee supplies to sell, as a gift. Again, I had not been able to pay them back the original amount that they had loaned me.

I was overwhelmed by the generosity of another friend who, upon receiving her Christmas bonus one year, took me shopping at the supermarket and paid for gas for my vehicle, before it was repossessed. Yes, I was astounded by her generosity because she was in the process of building her home and I knew that she was working for less than I was when I was employed.

When we went to the supermarket, I was shopping quite conservatively, in order to avoid running up her bill too much, as I secretly added up the cost of each item in my mind *(mental arithmetic)*.

Sometimes I would pass an item that I usually bought and deliberately not pick it up because I told myself there were other necessities that I had to get within her food bill budget. That did not miss her, though, because as I quietly passed by those items she would exclaim "Why didn't you take up X or Y or Z? I know you like that." It also surprised me how much she had retained about what I used. Then she would take the particular item down from the supermarket shelf and put it in the trolley (shopping cart).

Finally, we reached her stipulated food budget, since I was doing the math in my head. I told her so but she just nonchalantly said "You don't bother with that. You haven't picked up A and B and C as yet." I am eternally grateful to her for her generosity.

Yet another friend of mine, who lived in another part of the country, provided me with groceries on two separate occasions and money that her Mom sent for me on hearing of my situation. She thoughtfully provided every conceivable thing you would generally shop for – fresh fish and lambie (conch), various vegetables, provision, dried peas, detergent, bathing soap, olive oil and more. I was deeply touched by the fact that she had no transportation and travelled by bus with those heavy bags to get the groceries to me.

Later, I also had the support of some colleagues and friends who supported my coffee business as clients (See http://heidivincentgrenada.myorganogold.com/). There are others who helped in other small ways and at very crucial moments when I needed to 'keep my head above water'. To these persons, I am also very grateful.

In comparison to the few who went out of their way to help and support me in tremendous ways, there were countless others who couldn't care less, those who told me outright they could or would not help and those who simply pretended that life was normal with me.

I have recounted all of these stories of generous love and tangible support that I received from my very dear friends, in order to:

1. Let you know that you are not alone during this difficult time.

2. Guarantee you that God will send the right people to help you at just the right moments during your financial struggle.

3. Give you encouragement when you meet with similar experiences of denied help from family, friends and colleagues.

4. Prepare you for your new and clean beginning; what I call your fresh start in life, when it does come.

Once you come out of this financial challenge that you are facing right now, as a result of your unemployment situation, I want to strongly urge you to reach out and tangibly help others who may find themselves in the same situation that you are currently facing. **Don't forget where you have been!**

Saying that you will pray for someone facing the difficulty of financial stress and unemployment is just not good enough. For, as we are reminded in the Holy Bible:

"My friends, what good is it for one of you to say that you have faith if your actions do not prove it? Can that faith save you? Suppose there are brothers or sisters who need clothes and don't have enough to eat. What good is there in your saying to them, "God bless you! Keep warm and eat well!"- if you don't give them the necessities of life? So it is with faith: if it is alone and includes no actions, then it is dead" (James 2: 14 -17).

What YOU Can Do! – Get Started on Survivor Strategy No. 10

Apply the principle of swallowing pride and reaching out for help. Here's what I did and what you can do too:

1. Pray and ask God for the wisdom to know when and who to approach for help. *(You shouldn't ask for help until you really need it but do not wait too late either).*

2. Pray and ask God to reveal to each person whom you approach for help, how to help you specifically. *(No one person will give you all of*

the help you need or give it to you at the precise moment in which you need it; it's a collective effort).

3. Pray and ask God to show you how to wisely spend the funds (money) that you receive and successfully juggle it among your various financial obligations *(The financial help that you will receive will not solve your financial problem but it will keep you going for a while, if you allocate it wisely among your various debt obligations and spend it sparingly).*

4. A useful strategy for stretching the funds (money) that you receive is finding out the minimum allowable balance that you can have on your utility bills in order to avoid disconnection. For example, in my country, both the telephone and water companies will not disconnect your service if you have an outstanding balance of up to $50. The electricity company will allow you to be 2 months in arrears before sending you a disconnection notice.

May God bless you with wisdom to know when and who to ask for help!

Survivor Strategy 11
Purge Yourself of False Friends & Selfish Family

"It is during the worst times of your life that you will get to see the true colors of the people who say they care for you." ~ *Ritu Ghatourey*

So said, so done! I did get to experience for myself the true colors of the people who had over the years called themselves my friends and family.

As my financial situation grew worse, my vehicle was repossessed and I recall telling a so-called friend about it and to my utter shock and bewilderment he remained silent! **Silent!!!** Other friends and colleagues who knew about it had expressed their sympathy in various ways but no, this 'so-called' friend never uttered one word. It was during that strange, delayed and awkward silence that it slowly dawned on me that he had never wished me well.

Another person, with whom I am acquainted, was told by someone that my vehicle was repossessed. So when we met each other one day, she asked me, in a seemingly innocent enquiry and with a mocking smirk on her face, why I was no longer going to Church at a particular parish. I simply told her that I did not have my vehicle, without going into the details of it. Again she remained

71

silent. In her case, I know my honest answer left her without words. It was as if she was waiting for me to lie about my vehicle situation, so that she could have a good laugh behind my back knowing the details of my situation.

Yes! I know that, like me, you will be overwhelmed by the generosity of those who do help you, as well as shocked at the indifference of those who called themselves your friends prior to your financial demise.

As difficult a pill as it may be to swallow right now, I urge you to be thankful for this life experience which will help you to move forward with only the people who are your real friends and family and who truly care about you. Thank God for this 'hard' experience which will help you to naturally weed out the 'pretenders' in your life. **It is your blessing at this stage of your life!**

When my Dad died *(may he rest in peace)*, I felt that the only person who loved and truly cared for me had died. When I received no help from the other members of my family during my unemployment period, God consoled me with the account of Joseph's story in Genesis 37-45, when I kept asking Him why my family, who I loved dearly, was nowhere near in my time of need.

With the great outpouring of love that I received from my friends, who embraced and supported me like family, God showed me through the story of Joseph how to appreciate the good things that he was doing for me and providing for me in spite of my family's absence. I urge you to read the whole story of Joseph's life, especially if, like me, you have no support from any of your immediate family members during this difficult time in your life.

So now that you have been chastened by the knowledge of who your true friends and family are, you need to know how to purge yourself of those false friends and selfish family members, heal yourself and move forward joyously into the new future that God is carving out for you.

In order to rid myself of the hurt that I was experiencing at one point, I poured myself and all of my hurt feelings into an article that I wrote online titled, **'How to Purge Yourself of False Friends'** at http://heidivincent.hubpages.com/hub/how-to-purge-yourself-of-false-friends

You can read all about how to go about the process of cleansing yourself from those 'pretenders' and begin sloughing off the dead skin of the unproductive relationships that were clinging to you only because you were successful.

Apply the principle of purging yourself of false friends and selfish family. Here's what I did and what you can do too:

1. Express gratitude to God for the time they were a part of your life. *(I am sure you can think of at least one good thing that happened to you as a result of knowing them).*

2. Don't beat up on yourself! *(It serves you no good to waste time thinking about what you should have, could have or would have done differently).*

3. Protect yourself from those false friends and selfish family members, in the future, when things improve in your life *(For sure they will come 'buzzing' around again but you have to be strong and firmly keep them at bay).*

4. Move on with your life and don't be afraid to meet and befriend new people. *(Everybody is not the same and it's important that you remember this and use the lessons learnt to find good friends and friends who are like family).*

5. Learn the importance of having good friends. *(We all need good and supportive friends and family. So don't turn yourself into a hermit because of one*

or more bad experiences with false friends and selfish family members).

6. Learn the qualities of a good friend. *(The Holy Bible is full of examples of the various qualities that a good friend should possess. Review those qualities and apply them as criteria for the new friends that you will be making in the future).*

7. KEEP YOUR DREAMS and ASPIRATIONS TO YOURSELF!!! *(Only you can fully understand the gifts and talents that God has blessed you with and your true purpose in life).*

For more details on employing the purging principles, you can read my FREE article titled **'How to Purge Yourself of False Friends'** at http://heidivincent.hubpages.com/hub/how-to-purge-yourself-of-false-friends

May God bless you with true friends and loving family!

Survivor Strategy 12

Save big with Discount Cards, Coupons & Recyclable Products.

"A penny saved is a penny earned." ~ *Benjamin Franklin*

One day when my funds were extremely low, I was putting together some empty bottles, used egg cartoons and a discount (money back) cheque for $10 in order to make up money to buy some basic groceries, when I suddenly chuckled sadly to myself.

I chuckled because in that moment I felt like a beggar or 'piper' (drug addict) fighting to pull together enough change. I chuckled because I think I had still been able to maintain a sense of humour in a situation that was no laughing matter. It was a melancholic chuckle, though, because in my mind I could not believe that I was now experiencing such financial poverty.

At that time, I also made a point of using each and every discount card to get all available discounts anywhere I had to shop. The discounts on these various cards ranged from 5 percent to 7 and a half percent. I also registered for shopper's point cards, where you could redeem accumulated points for cash at a later date. Believe me, it all does add up and come in very handy, as I myself experienced with that $10 discount (money back) cheque which helped to get me enough spending power to get by at that crucial moment.

In some countries, I know that persons are able to cut out and redeem coupons on food packaging. This was not an available option in my country but if it is, in your country, then I urge you to seriously consider making use of coupons in order to meet your grocery expenses. No matter how seemingly small or insignificant, it all adds up.

During especially festive seasons such as Christmas, the supermarkets often gave customers one or more ticket-like stubs to fill out and place in a box for a chance to win a food hamper in a raffle, based on the dollar amount of the groceries purchased. When I was working, I remember receiving several of these but I saw it as a harassment to fill out all of my details on each of those ticket stubs and so I just never bothered with them.

However, during one Christmas season, while I was unemployed and shopping at my regular supermarket, I was given one of those ticket-stubs to fill out. Since I was looking for any and every legal opportunity to take advantage of, I took the time to fill it out and placed it in the indicated raffle box with a prayer in my heart that I would win one of the food hampers.

To my utter surprise, I did win one of the food hampers! This was a hamper with a difference, though. It was worth $500 but you had to do some 'speed shopping' for groceries up to an amount of $500 that the supermarket would pay for. The way the 'speed shopping' works is that you are given a certain amount of minutes to 'fly' around the supermarket with a trolley (shopping cart) and pick up groceries up to the value of $500. I had only seen it done on television before and in reality I enjoyed the excitement of it.

The challenge is to maximize the shopping time given, so that you can get the maximum amount of dollars' worth of groceries, up to the limit of $500, before your shopping time runs out. I was GOOD at this 'speed shopping'!!! My groceries came up to only a few dollars short of the $500 limit. My simple success trick was to avoid scampering around the supermarket on the actual day by:

1. Working out a careful but short list of the items that I used most frequently (*I wrote it down on paper first and then memorized it in my head. Fewer items meant less stops*).

2. Memorizing each shopping lane carefully and the specific lanes on which the items that I would be picking up were located (*If you know exactly which*

lanes you need to go to beforehand, then this also saves you time).

3. Picking up items in bulk and large sizes, as well as items that did not have short shelf life or near expiry dates, such as toilet paper, detergent for washing, rice, flour, sugar, olive oil, cooking oil, etc. *(These were all items that could not go to waste since they were the items used most frequently).*

God had once again supplied my needs in a most unusual way! At a time when $50 in groceries was a huge bill for me, I had received $500 worth of free groceries.

During another Christmas season, while I was unemployed, I again won another food hamper. This one comprised a salted ham, though, which I could not use. It did come in handy, however, since I was able to give it to a friend of mine for her Christmas lunch, to which she had invited me and some of her close friends and family.

I also saved some money by purchasing newly expired items in the supermarkets. Newly expired items in supermarkets are often kept for a little while with a 'reduced price' sticker on them. These items are usually still good for at least one month after the stated expiry date.   This is another great way to reduce your food bill and save money.

I also purchased the 'in-house' brand of a certain supermarket which guaranteed the shopper that in whatever section of the supermarket the brand name was found, the item would be cheaper than all the other brands. This was always true and worked out to as much as $1 and cents cheaper, which is a lot when added up.

No name items, which are loosely packed by supermarkets, also provide great savings for shoppers.

Supermarkets also have weekly specials on certain items. You just need to look for the designated sticker of tab on the respective supermarket shelves. So be sure to make use of all of these savings opportunities.

What YOU Can Do! – Get Started on Survivor Strategy No. 12

Apply the principle of using the potential savings from Discount Cards, Coupons, Recyclable Products, In-house brands, Newly Expired Items & Weekly Specials. Here's what I did and what you can do too:

1. Apply for and use all available cash discount or point accumulation cards that are being offered by supermarkets and other businesses whose services

you use often *(Signing up for the cards is free in most instances; there are no charges or fees)*.

2. Sell back recyclable products, such as bottles, egg cartons and other containers. *(A few cents on each eventually adds up. Don't let pride get in your way)*.

3. Cut out all redeemable coupons from food packaging and redeem them for cash or additional food products *(Even if you end up with plenty of one thing, take them and search for creative and new ways of preparing food that will use those ingredients, so that you don't get fed up of eating the same thing all the time)*.

4. Be on the lookout for weekly specials and discounts on selected supermarket items.

5. Search for expired items with reduced pricing, both on items that you use regularly and those that you use infrequently *(This is pure 'luck & chance'. Once when I really needed butter but did not have enough to buy it at the regular price, by divine intervention from God, I happened to be in the supermarket on the very day that there was only ONE 16 ounce packet of Anchor butter at reduced pricing. I nearly did a cartwheel in the supermarket)*.

6. Take part in any promotions, giveaways or raffles being offered by your supermarket *(You never*

know when it will be your turn to become a winner!).

May God grant you wisdom in your spending!

Survivor Strategy 13
Continue to Tithe.

> *"I ask you, is it right for a person to cheat God? Of course not, yet you are cheating me. 'How?' you ask. In the matter of tithes and offerings...Bring the full amount of your tithes to the Temple, so that there will be plenty of food there. Put me to the test and you will see that I will open the windows of heaven and pour out on you in abundance all kinds of good things"* ~ *Malachi 3:6-12*

With already limited finances, tithing seems like a bad joke...Right? I know! Back when I was fully employed and working for a very good salary that was much higher than what my average countryman/woman earned, I dutifully paid my tithes. I was able to comfortably give my tithes, meet all of my monthly obligations, save and splurge on entertainment with some of my salary.

During my unemployment period, however, I grappled constantly with this tithing principle because money was so scarce that every cent I got was already spent by the time I received it. I would talk to God about whether I really had to tithe during that period, since I always needed more than I was receiving.

Then two things happened! Firstly, in my daily reading of the Holy Bible, I came across the story of the widow's mite in Mark 12:41 – 44, wherein Jesus compared the offering/tithes of a rich man who put lots of money in the Temple treasury and a poor widow who gave only two copper coins that were equivalent to a penny.

In the story, Jesus explained that although the widow's offering/tithes was small in monetary value compared to the rich man's offering/tithes, it far surpassed the rich man's offering because while he was giving from his surplus, she gave all of the little that she had.

It was as if God had given me the opportunity to step back and see myself as both the rich man and the poor widow during my lifetime. As the rich man, during my working life, I had no problem giving of my surplus but as the poor widow, during my period of unemployment, I was ashamed of my stinginess before God. The poor widow was far nobler than I was in my current unemployment situation. Up until that point, I couldn't spare God one penny because I argued with Him that I needed it all.

Secondly, I read one of the readings from 'The Secret Scrolls' that sounded a lot like the Bible principle in Luke 6:38, which I will share with you near the end of this chapter:

"Tithing is a powerful way to revolutionize your mind about money; the very act of tithing says that there is plenty of money, because you're giving some away. As a consequence, it will increase the flow of money and all good things into your life. And, you will discover that the joy and happiness you receive in return is far beyond the monetary value of what you gave." *(Rhonda Byrne, 'The Secret Scrolls – The Way Out of Financial Struggle')*

So I changed my perspective on tithing, during my unemployment period, and I began to wholeheartedly give God his due from whatever I received. The reality of how much I owed and how much I needed each and every cent that I received was always looming large in my head whenever I received money. However, I maintained that discipline of tithing by reminding myself that the first portion of my earnings was not mine. It belonged to God and anything else but giving it to God was tantamount to stealing from God.

Tithing should possess three key qualities. Firstly, it should come from your first fruits or your very best *(Numbers 18:21)*. Secondly, it should be done willingly *(Acts 5:1-11)*. Thirdly, it should be done generously *(2 Corinthians 9)*.

Some churches have a stipulated percentage amount of ten percent (10%), as in the Old Testament, which should be set aside and given as tithes. However, the Catholic Church, of which I am a member, does not have a stipulated fixed amount or percentage for tithing.

Irrespective of which religious denomination you belong to, if your tithes are given from your best, and your

87

tithing is also done both willingly and generously, then you can be assured that, like Abel *(Genesis 4)*, your tithes will be pleasing to God.

The tithes that you give to the Church are usually used to take care of the priests/ministers, cover church expenses and look after the poor and underprivileged.

So, there are two ways that you can tithe. Firstly, you can give all of your tithes to your Church. By doing this, you will be helping to upkeep your priests and religious ministers, similar to how the Israelites supported the Aaronite priests *(Leviticus 7, 8 & 10)* and the Levite priests *(Numbers 18: 25-32)* by giving them a portion of the food offerings.

Secondly, you can give a portion of your tithes to the Church and give the balance to one or more charities, such as St. Vincent de Paul, which help the poor, underprivileged, disabled and differently abled, since we are reminded that we should:

> *"Give to others, and God will give to you. Indeed, you will receive a full measure, a generous helping, poured into your hands—all that you can hold. The measure you use for others is the one that God will use for you." ~ Luke 6:38*

What YOU Can Do! – Get Started on Survivor
Strategy No. 13

**Apply the principle of giving God his due by tithing
always.** Here's what I did and what you can do too:

1. Set aside one tenth of any income that you
   receive for God or whatever generously fixed
   amount the Holy Spirit directs you to set aside
   *(Never begin by calculating all the bills you
   have to pay and other financial obligations that
   you have to meet or else you will never have
   enough to give God).*

2. Think of worthy charities, ordinary or special
   causes, that you can give a portion of your
   tithes to or a particular person or family in
   need. *(Ask the Holy Spirit to direct you about
   how, how much and to whom or what cause you
   should give the decided portion of your tithes
   to).*

May you be moved always to give back to God, from
whatever you receive, willingly, generously and from
your very best!

Survivor Strategy 14
Make Wise Financial Decisions and Don't Think That Your Life Has Ended or Contemplate Ending Your Life, Even if You Lose Your Money &/or Property

> *"Property may be destroyed and money may lose its purchasing power; but, character, health, knowledge and good judgement will always be in demand under all conditions" ~ Roger Babson*

With the loss of my job, and my mortgage, vehicle, credit union and credit card loan obligations looming large each month, I soon 'fell into hot water'. Additionally, my bank was not budging, in terms of reducing my monthly payments on my mortgage and vehicle loans, so as time rolled by I had moved from just barely making the monthly payments to catching up on interest payments to paying a small part of the monthly mortgage payment towards my principal sporadically *(about every 4 months)*.

When a bailiff served me papers, took the keys for my vehicle and drove away with my vehicle, it broke my heart! I cried incessantly for a whole night and the following day because one and a half years from that date, I would have completed my vehicle loan payments and owned my vehicle free and clear of any debt.

Losing my vehicle was really difficult for me, since I did not live near the main road at that time and a trip to anywhere – the city, the post office, the supermarket – meant that I had to first walk half mile to the bus stop on the main road. In spite of the distance, walking out from my home was not that bad but walking in was always difficult, since I would be exhausted after spending nearly the whole day walking around looking for sales and loaded up with groceries or my coffee and tea products.

The buses would drop you halfway inside the road where I lived, if you asked, for an additional charge of $5. But at that time $5 was too much to spend on such a luxury, since it was almost the full amount of a round trip to the city *(The bus fare one way was $3.25; a total of $6.50 round trip)*.

As I struggled to build my customer base for my coffee business in the first two year of business, there were days when I would not get one box of coffee or tea sold. On days when I did not sell any products, I had to walk back home loaded up with all of the products that I had originally walked out with. My shoulders and back ached terribly from carrying around all of that load and I would most times just bathe and fall right into my bed exhausted to the bone.

Prior to having my vehicle repossessed, I had substantial savings at two commercial banks, two credit unions and three other investment companies. As my unemployment situation dragged on and my financial position worsened, I watched helplessly as my mortgage loan payment swallowed up my savings and investments.

First my bank savings account moved below the minimum balance and for a while I had to painfully watch as the bank deducted $10 each month, as a result of me having a constant balance below the minimum amount. Then it just made no sense at all to hold any money in the bank. So I had to return to the old time days of holding whatever money I came by under my mattress.

At the same time, I was unwisely using my credit card to meet other bills as they came due because I kept telling myself that I would soon find employment or a really good consultancy opportunity, I'd pay off the credit card loan and things would be back to normal again.

However, as first the months, then the years rolled by and my financial situation worsened, payments became few and far between on my loan obligations. With my debt piled high and increasingly scarce income, I began to dread receiving calls from the bank and the credit union, who were continuously calling to find out when I would rectify my loan situation. I developed instant headaches on those occasions when I received calls because I could never really provide any specifics about when I would be able to make another payment, since I was officially unemployed.

After repeated calls from the credit union, they sent a bailiff to serve me papers for my outstanding debt to them.

Then I was served court papers by a bailiff, at my home, in relation to my mortgage with the bank. I had to appear in court in three months' time, since the bank had finally made a claim against my home. My worst fear had been realized! I felt totally defeated! I didn't want to fight anymore.

I can't say that I cried. It was more like tears poured from my eyes, because I felt so defeated that there was no effort on my part to cry. All of the anguish of my soul just overwhelmed me and poured itself out, because God alone knew how much I had kept bottled up inside of me while trying to keep things together financially, mentally and emotionally.

I did eventually get up from my crying and depression and do what was necessary.

In my professional life, prior to becoming unemployed, I was a Portfolio Manager employed with a prominent mutual fund company, where I successfully managed millions of dollars for customers. I was also an Assistant Dean and Associate Professor at a renowned university, where I taught courses in business and finance. I have also made numerous wise investments for myself and on behalf of my company's clients. So the financial advice that I will be sharing with you at the end of this chapter is tried, tested and true!

What YOU Can Do! – Get Started on Survivor Strategy No. 14

Apply the principle of making wise financial decisions, as well as acknowledging and embracing the fact that you have worth beyond the property that you own. Here's what I did and what you can do:

1. Pray and ask God for guidance before making each and every financial decision *(God ALWAYS provides guidance in whatever area of our lives that we seek his assistance, including our finances. Remember, He blessed many people in the Bible with wealth. God wants to bless your finances as well)*.

2. Approach the bank or financial institution with which you have your vehicle, mortgage or other loans, in order to work out a reduced monthly or

other periodic payment plan, while you 'get back on your feet' and recover from your unemployment situation and the resultant financial challenges. *(My bank was very uncooperative in this regard but there are many other banks and financial institutions that are willing to work with customers).*

3. Pay a little towards each of your debt obligations from whatever money you receive, whenever you receive it *(Paying something, no matter how small, serves to appease some debtors, since they will see that you are making a conscious effort to make repayments despite your challenging circumstances).*

4. Avoid using your credit card to meet monthly expenses. *(Credit card debt quickly adds up and even if you are able to make the minimum monthly payment, the majority of that payment goes towards interest which is usually very high – 60% or more. So your actual principal balance only goes down by a tiny bit. And since interest is calculated on that principal balance, your interest payments, and by extension your minimum balance, will remain high and it will take you forever to pay off your credit card debt. This is great for the bank but terrible for you!).*

5. Each time you get money, as little as it is and as difficult as it may be to stretch your funds any further, try to pay a little more than the minimum balance on your credit card *(The extra amount that you pay over the minimum balance will go towards reducing your principal balance and you will eventually notice your principal balance drop significantly).*

6. Try to sell your vehicle or home before the bank repossesses it *(If you sell your own home or vehicle, you have control over the selling price. If the bank repossesses and sells your home or vehicle, on the other hand, the bank most times sells it at less than its true value, since the bank is primarily interested in making back what is owed by you on the vehicle or house.*

The first six (6) strategies that I have outlined above, in this chapter, are tailored to assist you with making wise financial decisions while you are unemployed.

The following seven (7) strategies are geared towards helping you make wise financial decisions once you begin to climb out of your unemployment situation and start generating steady income streams once again.

7. Join a credit union and consider saving and, eventually taking whatever future loans you require from that credit union instead of from a bank *(Because credit unions are member-owned, unlike banks, they are more willing to negotiate payments when you encounter a financial crisis and they usually do not charge you a daily late payment charge, like the bank. This daily late payment charge is what usually ends up crippling mortgagor's who have fallen behind on their payments and enables the bank to quickly lay claim to your property that you have pledged as security)*.

8. Develop the discipline of putting a fixed percentage of your income towards savings *(In fact, I would suggest this order of allocating all the monies that you receive. Firstly, set aside your 10%, or whatever percentage, tithes to God. Secondly, set aside a fixed percentage to go towards savings. Thirdly, you can pay your bills and countless obligations. The ideal savings percentage is 20% of your income but as you are recovering from unemployment, this will prove extremely difficult. So I would advise you to start with as small an amount as $20 and gradually increase to a small fixed percentage, like 3% and then work your way up to that ideal 20%, as your financial position improves)*.

9. Place only a minimal amount of your savings at the bank and the majority of your savings at a credit union and/or an investment company.

10. Follow the age old, wise principle of not putting all of your eggs in one basket when you save *(Look around for investment opportunities that offer slightly higher returns than a bank savings account. Fixed Deposits (Certificates of Deposit), Mutual Funds and Special Credit Union Savings Plans are usually very safe investment opportunities that will earn you a decently higher interest rate over your regular bank savings account.*

    DO NOT invest in investment opportunities – which I call 'schemes' – that promise you excessively high returns. If it sounds too good to be true, it normally is and that's your first powerful cue to stay away from such an investment 'scheme').

11. Always reinvest a portion of the interest that you earn on your savings and investment accounts *(Let's suppose that you invested $10,000 in a 5% Fixed Deposit/Certificate of Deposit for one year. At the end of the one year, when you receive the original principal amount of $10,000 and the interest of $500 earned on the Fixed*

Deposit/Certificate of Deposit, consider reinvesting a portion of that $500).

12. Break up your savings and investment accounts according to your specific goals in the short, medium and long-term *(What I mean by this is that you may want to set aside some funds for furthering your education, your children's education, buying a home or buying a car or for your retirement. If you keep all of your savings in one account, as the amount increases, I may tempt you to borrow from it as you see the large sum piled up in your account.*

    If, however, your savings is separated out into different accounts with differing maturity dates, you are likely to remain disciplined and realistic about the amount that is still needed to reach each of your goals and not 'borrow' from those accounts.

13. When investing in Fixed Deposits (Certificates of Deposit), split up the entire amount that you are investing into Fixed Deposits with varying maturities *(3 months, 6 months, 9 months, 1 year, 2 years, or whatever other maturity terms are being offered by your financial institution.)*

    It is important to note that financial institutions often give you a reduced amount on your investment if you redeem a Fixed

Deposit/Certificate of Deposit before its maturity date.

So, if an emergency arises that necessitates you dipping into your savings or investment, if you have several Fixed Deposits with varying maturity terms, you can choose to redeem only one or two, for example, so that you will not lose too much interest overall. You will only lose some interest on the one or two Fixed Deposits that were redeemed early, while keeping your other investments intact. This would not be the case if you had only one Fixed Deposit and had to redeem the whole amount early, in order to use some of it for your emergency).

Before I move on to the next chapter, I want to leave you with a powerful Bible promise from our loving God:

"When you pass through deep waters, I will be with you;
your troubles will not overwhelm you.
When you pass through fire, you will not be burned;
the hard trials that come will not hurt you." *(Isaiah 43:2)*

May God bless you with financial wisdom!

Survivor Strategy 15
Trust God as Your Provider

> *"And with all his abundant wealth through Christ Jesus, my God will supply all your needs."*
> *~ Philippians 4:19*

ENOUGH! That's the word I would use to accurately describe how God provided for me during my period of unemployment.

Having been accustomed in my life to plenty, it was now quite humbling and, at first, nerve racking, to just have enough and no excess. If I got something to do or God moved a friend to help me, then it would be just enough to pay this bill or that bill. There's a certain sense of security one feels with excess cash that I no longer felt.

On one occasion, I went to the city to drop of a box of tea for a client. However, when I arrived in the city and called the client so that we could meet, he indicated that he did not have his cheque book with him, so that I would have to come back another day. Not only was this disappointing but it left me without much needed funds that I was expecting from that sale.

As I sat in the bus that would take me home, I remember speaking to God in my mind and telling Him how disappointed I was and asking for His help, since I only had enough money to get home and back into the city on another day but not enough to get back home on that other day, whenever it would be.

As the bus filled up with passengers, the tout (bus conductor) hustled for the last passenger and, lo and behold, a friend of mine, who lived in a totally different part of the country from me, got onto the bus. After exchanging greetings, she told me that she was taking her daughter to see a particular doctor who was en route to my home. When the bus arrived at her destination, she paid the bus conductor the requisite bus fare for herself, her daughter and me.

As soon as I reached home, I called her to thank her and explain how much her gesture meant to me. It now meant that I had the bus fare for a round trip to the city and back home on the next occasion that I had to go into the city.

On another occasion, I was so exhausted by my lack of finances and with no sight of potential income as the month ended, I simply prayed asking God to provide for me during the following month. A friend of mine called to say that she had bought some groceries for me and was calling to make arrangements for us to meet in the city for me to collect it. She paid for my bus fare to and from the city, as well as the extra fare into the area where I lived, since I was loaded up with her blessing of groceries.

On yet another occasion, as I was walking from my home to the public bus stop on the main road, I prayed asking God to provide transportation for me on the second leg of my journey. When I reached the bus stop on the main road, an old school teacher of mine passed by and gave me a ride in his vehicle.

As we were nearing the city, I asked where he was going to, so that I would know where to get off. He indicated where he was going, which was in the opposite direction to my final destination. Then he enquired about my final destination. When I told him, he simply said that he would give me a ride there. I thanked him profusely, since, as I explained previously, it was clearly out of his way. I was blown away by God's provision in my life once again.

On one occasion, I badly needed flour but I just did not have enough to get it at the supermarket after picking up a few other more essential items. So I came home without it but made a mental note to get it whenever I received any other source of income. About a day or 2 later, my neighbour called me to tell me that she had something for me. When I opened what she gave me, I could not believe it; it was a 5 pound bag of baking flour.

Since I was unemployed for more than five years, I can recount an endless list of circumstances when God provided for me. I have communicated only some of those instances for you in this chapter and throughout the book for the sake of time and space.

However, take to heart and seriously apply the scripture verse in **Matthew 7:7-8**, *"Ask, and you will receive; seek, and you will find; knock, and the door will be opened to you. For everyone who asks will receive, and anyone who seeks will find, and the door will be opened to those who knock"*.

Notice that action is required on your part in the first sentence and then there is a clear promise that if you do the actions you will get results. It does not say for how long we are to ask, seek or knock. Experience has shown, though, that many of us stop asking, seeking and knocking too early, which is why we do not receive the promised results.

In **Luke 18:1-6**, we are told that Jesus specifically "…told his disciples [The Parable of the Widow and the Judge] to teach them that they should always pray and never become discouraged". Notice, when you read the parable, it was the persistence of the widow that eventually got her what she wanted from the Judge – justice. Likewise, we should never stop asking, seeking and knocking at Heaven's door until we get a response from God.

Before I end this chapter, however, I strongly urge you to follow Edgar Page Stites' advice on trusting Jesus, also:

Trusting Jesus
Simply trusting every day,
Trusting through a stormy way;
Even when my faith is small,
Trusting Jesus, that is all.

Singing if my way is clear;
Praying if the path is drear;
If in danger, for Him call;
Trusting Jesus, that is all.
[by Edgar Page Stites (1836 - 1921)]

What YOU Can Do! – Get Started on Survivor Strategy No. 15

Apply the principle of fully trusting God as the provider of all your needs. Here's what I did and what you can do too:

1. Read scripture verses from the Holy Bible, daily, which will reminder you that God is willing to

help you and will help you *(Matthew 6:24-34, Psalm 9:9, Psalm 37:3-5, Psalm 46:1-3, Psalm 84: 11-12, Psalm 91:15, Psalm 125:1 Proverbs 3:5-6, Romans 8:28, Philippians 4:19, 1 Peter 5:7 & more)*.

2. Read the various stories and accounts in the Holy Bible of the many instances that God provided for His people, beginning with Adam and Eve in Genesis *(Try as hard as you can not to look at or dwell on what you are not seeing in the physical, in terms of your situation improving. Amaze God with your faith, as Jesus was amazed by the faith of the centurion (Matthew 8: 5-13), who believed that Jesus could heal his servant by simply speaking the words of healing and not even visiting his home or touching his servant)*.

3. Practice saying affirmations like those I have outlined in chapter 8 (Survivor Strategy 8) repeatedly, in order to remind yourself that God knows your needs and will supply them in exactly the right time.

Just so you don't forget, as things 'seem' to worsen, let me remind you in the powerful words of the first verse and refrain of the song **'God Will Take Care of You'**, which was written by Civilla D. Martin and to which her husband, Walter. S. Martin, put the music:

Heidi E. Vincent

Be not dismayed whate'er betide,
God will take care of you;
Beneath His wings of love abide,
God will take care of you.

God will take care of you,
Through every day. O'er all the way.
He will take care of you.
God will take care of you.

May you trust always in God's provision and may He supply all of your needs in His perfect timing!

Epilogue
Keep Trying, Never Quit & Never Give Up!!!

As we are so appropriately reminded by Billy Graham, *"The Christian life is not a constant high. I have my moments of deep discouragement. I have to go to God in prayer with tears in my eyes, and say, 'O God, forgive me,' or 'Help me.'"*.

The same is true of life in general, even if you are not a Christian; there is no constant high. Likewise your current low period will come to an end.

I can't tell you for how long after reading this book that your unemployment, underemployment or sporadic employment situation will continue. Perhaps, it will end today, maybe in a few weeks' time or a lot of months later. What I do know for sure is that if you apply the unemployment survivor principles/strategies that I have shared with you, you will eventually find yourself in a better place financially and otherwise.

In retrospect, this terribly painful period of unemployment, underemployment or irregular employment in your life will be one of your greatest blessings, because:

"It is in the quiet crucible of your personal, private suffering that your noblest dreams are born and God's greatest gifts are given in compensation for what you've been through." ~
Wintley Phipps

I hope that you have been comforted, even if it is in some small way, by me sharing my very own unemployment story with you. I have also shared with you several specific steps/actions/activities that you can do in order to climb out of your current unemployment, underemployment or sporadic employment situation.

You can start anywhere you want. You don't have to do things in the order that they are listed here either. Just do like Dr. King wisely advises below:

"Take the first step in faith. You don't have to see the whole staircase. Just take the first step." ~
Dr. Martin Luther King Jr. (1929-1968)